I0816858

RAFTING
INTO THE
AFTER-
LIFE

awe
tumbled
autumn
bled

MIKHAIL HOROWITZ

42 POEMS FROM **ONE YEAR**

CODHILL PRESS
NEW PALTZ, NEW YORK

ACKNOWLEDGEMENTS

Three of these poems (1.5, 2.11, 8.30) first appeared in *Hunger* magazine (ed. J. J. Blickstein, Vol. 1, No. 3, 1998).

The poems titled 1.17 and 4.8 first appeared in the *Woodstock Journal* (ed. Ed Sanders, January and April, 1997). The same newspaper also published earlier versions (fragments of the fragments) of the poems titled 1.1, 1.5, 1.26, 4.22, 10.14, 10.15, 10.23 in 1997.

This is a chapbook published by Codhill Press.

ISBN 1-930337-33-7
Cover art by Carol Zaloom. Frontispiece by the author. Design by Carla Rozman.
Manufactured in the United States of America. First Edition.

FOR **CAROL ZALOOM**, EVERY DAY OF THE YEAR

1.1

Datsun beeps
Subaru passes
—sound of the water

(& already I hear them humming:
iotas & moments of the coming year

fragments gathering into one big fragment & coalescing
with bits & pieces of personal history,   yester-shreds

shards of shattered memory
to re-remember here)

must remember to thank her, for distracting me from
whatever noble purposes I might have fallen prey to

not that it should all cohere, but
that it should
sing, & singing
bring its fresh
connections near

something that is of shards the Chartres

of scraps the Taj

of jottings the Acropolis

of calendars the Alamo

1.5

Against doctor's orders
she's going to town for
"Noxzema, *Foucault's Pendulum*, and vodka."

His big plan's to stay
in bed, concocting Zen
knock-knock jokes, e.g.:

No knocks.
Who's not there?
Not me.
Not me who?
Not me the moon in the branches

1.17

What a view from the
deck, you can almost rise &
fly to the distant ridge, over
the valley & silvery lens of the
reservoir, winging above the oaks &
snowy pines, into the blue
stillness that is really an immense
hum, the humming of something impersonal
& remote, unrealized & inviolable, distinct
from yet fully encompassing the endless
drone of motors, long whistles & tiny
cries, bird calls & car
horns, hysterical sirens &
intimate conversations, clacking
of heaters & creak of a wheelchair
occupied only by light in the
noonday studio

1.26

cock burning when I piss at midnight, gone by morning
(the burning, not the cock)

dissolving into the
twined sigh of wind
chimes

dissolving into ordinary jazz

(bassist scatting as he sculpts
arpeggios, whittling that big stick
down to a Q-tip, digging out the wax
from inner ear)

still, I'm nullius fillius
nobody's child
the law can't touch me
at all

tho according to M.,
"There's Law, & there's Policy.
Policy is greater than Law.
Policy determines how the Law is enforced,
& who benefits from the Law."

not the bassist, who's
later debased & busted
for a J

but music continues, unbustable & unabated

hauling wood in icy downpour
listen to it hissing in the stove

2.10

she looked so stunning as
she almost ran me down in
the parking lot

augury of that dark event
whose hub we are

Finnegans Wake: the book ain't over 'til the fat Liffey sings

My mind, he says, is a leg trap,
& if I get caught, I can chew it off
at the cerebellum

& she strains to hear him, as

high above the frozen creek
a train whistle whitens the
snow

2.11

it's about language, not about feelings

yet all these people
insisting it be about
feelings, if that's
the case let's just
replace Mayakovsky
with Barry Manilow

& it's not even *about* anything, any more

than a tree is about
anything or a person
& his/her life is
about anything more
or less than a localized
expression of some oceanic
monstrosity, a momentary
flare of star-stuff
dressed in flesh

& once again I've nothing to wear.

frozen stars, cold tinkle
of wind chimes on the white porch of
a funeral home

2.24

rubbed her back in the
hospital, her fugitive
cigarette,   the last
ash, let it go

total negation: a nice place to
visit, but I'd rather not spend
Eternity there

black branches limned in white, the oaks & pines in a
fine mist of sighs, the forest a frosty murmur, a tufted
whisper, a formal soliloquy of rime

in medias res

you try to take
a breath, & notice
things, & let them
speak for them-
selves

sometimes you get in the
way, but sometimes in an
interesting way

3.2

Q: When is a poem finished

(visit her with a bottle
of *sake,* bamboo flutes &
tax forms

& teetering home
alone, electric lights &
wires humming the note B

& that's why it's so hard, he says, to end
a movie, or to end it satisfactorily; even
with a bad movie, one feels the action was
going before it started, & continues after
the credits

& harmonizing now with
lights & wires, I'm hum-
ming as I slowly come a-

part, readying the empty
set for bed)

A: When I can't possibly make it any worse

3.22

solitary bird, singing
so faintly at daybreak

soon
the whole
mishpocheh's
up & gushing

but it might as well be 3 a.m. for her,
who mourns "the death of the physical universe"
of his body, which has abandoned hers for a 23-
year-old Cherman chippie in Belize

cheap wine & dear company, &
our talk encompasses the failure of labels, the
uses of rage, the giddiness that often accompanies
a particularly strenuous repression of sexual energy

Victoria's Secret: that the
models are sacrificial, & inter-
changeable

even by broad daylight,
we stack wood under the Pleiades

3.29

guess it's just destined to end like so:
two ships passing in the behavioral sink

(her last salvo, directed against the restaurant
purporting to serve "authentic Caribbean cuisine"

e.g., chicken killed at your
table by the waitress,
Epiphany Proudfoot)

out to the swollen brook, to forget about it

remember the nature of flux, to keep fluxing

water
remembers me,
but
not as "me"

4.8

a-shimmer with hymns
the church at the corner

Easter
she says
is the freshness

nothing to do with a man
or a man-god

it is a woman whose
light touch flutters the blue
plastic wrappings of dockside

boats, wakens the friendly
yellow, the tentative halo
of april daisies

4.13

says Joe, *Don't give 'em anything they can hum*

privilege or luck, to dine upon
this ineluctable duck, with wild
mushroom smashed potatoes, pearl
onions & dusky jus, & heavenly
crème brûlée

lying naked with 3 cats, four muzzy mammals, purring
like furry engines, blurred abed

&
even in
a stopped car moving
so fast her
mind before the light
changed

Hey, cried the cop
Stop & dig the dithyrambs on that forsythia!

4.22

he calls falafels "feeling awfuls"

& later buys me a coupla hot dogs "made from dead winos" at
Nathan's Remains

even so, it is still spring, &

one, two, three, for-
sythia in a lemony hedge, a
mustard eruption

& moonrise, a pear soaked in wine
Chateau Hecate, c. 1400 B.C.

5.5

ars longa, tsuris brevis

fresh from seeing her shrink, she's terrified & horny

not necessarily in that order

we stand there watching the cat in the litter box

quickly in & quickly out

we

sense the aspen

tingling in the

dark

5.6

big cloud, God with a bulbous nose

passing up there where *I* should be, instead
of stuck in this dumpster, listening with a
handicap to the Holland Tunnel Chamber
Jazz Quartet

ah well, what more to say
we wrinkled the wrong way

even as I hail
the wild azaleas

those nameless yellow blooms
have already faded, down by the
brook in the woods

5.29

Huge purply bruises constellate the welkin of my ankle, but
I can hobble again!

so hobbling & monogamous, into the sunset with a thud, into
oblivion with a rickety rictus, Homo

derelictus, I tell her I've never taken her for granted yet
everything is tinged with inevitability, like

a dappled deer on a dappled road, dappling into the margins
of driver's consciousness

5.31

land's end, everything flaps:

the flags
the windsocks
the gossiping mouths of gulls

at his funeral, the irony of bad art on the walls

& remembering her wedding, she in bride's white & spit-
curls, & the groom's mother in a wheelchair, wizened in
spirit, & Celtic harpist they hired to strum them in, &
just as they entered the clearing to gentle glissandos,
the only puff of the stifling, sultry, insufferable day
played lightly in the branches, showering the wedding
guests with blossoms

walking wood's edge
with pine wand as a
fly whisk, thinking

I've wasted my life

6.9

fucked me fiercely, on top

like a tiger born in the year of the horse

and now the moment's run its murderous course

and now this breeze

rippling the indifferent moon

obscured by trees

6.22

preceding
& postdating

a late improvisation
on the cloven sopranino

the grinding of cicadas
the thrumming of numberless
bugs

that evening
3 poets reading poetry over pesto

not to hear the droning of our own voices
but the silences in between

(& what was her take on Medusa?
that her so-called victims were
in fact victimized by their own
inability to feel; that behold-
ing the Gorgon, the Dark Mother,
without acknowledging her as central
to the life of the Soul, they turned
themselves to stone)

6.29

ordinary car key in sun's glare a burning ingot
ordinary alchemy

she offers to buy me a glass of wine & all I can do is cry
it's anti-hunky-dory

but settling fly does not disturb the turtle
& then a windfall apple in country graveyard

(all of it a gift, even the things we pay for)

& at noon
where I kneeled

mosaic of brown cow pies
in the field

this weighty head
becoming its husk

one crow flies
above it   towards dusk

7.2

in slanting light
barn slats turn to
stalactites when I
squint

cicada diminuendos in the day lilies, &

guitarist strumming
sultry tunes by Luis
Bonfa, as great blue
gift of a heron lofts
over, lifted from
great blue hills

indoors, a fire-

fly lands on my pants, vigils there, a
lighthouse on my thigh

Perceiving is believing?
Perception obviates need for belief.
This hath the water taught me, imparting
King James diction into the bargain.

7.6

ah, these binges of self-denial

lying with her
in a blueberry patch &
doing nothing, as promiscuous
flies & insatiable gnats have
their ways with us

ever the unwelcome interventionist, I save
a mouse from a cat

a sultry, humid, gravid day

air dense the landscape fra diavolo

clouds are crepuscular voluptuaries
good for nothing, what better to be
good for?

7.21

at the museum
silence of distilled time

a magnified silence that separates us
from all these distant lives in dioramas

& driving upstate in cenozoic rain
frogs hop into oncoming headlights

instant squish & it's back to the
carboniferous

& finally home a cricket in the bookcase
chirping to William Blake & Bobbie Burns

8.7

the world to be is combustible gumbo

& *friendship,* says Proust, *is a delusion,*
but two with the same contempt for it can
be a comfort to each other

& all this time as friends
dropped off, I thought there were none on me,
but

here now
the flies

— silversmithed bodies & buggy red eyes —

alighting on
thumbs & knuckles
as I write

8.13

spider & wasp, locked in a deadly debate

pushing each other up & down the pane, apache dancers

as for us, we trek this mud sans metaphor

on we slog, churning up ridges & furrows of mush-gush

as C. tells me that Lucy, our remotest appellated ancestor,
was so named because *Lucy in the Sky with Diamonds* was
playing when they found her bones

why haven't they found her freckles, her favorite dress

why haven't they found her pills, her purse, her phones

8.21

a year ago today
those confectionery groans in the apartment above
— chocolatey hoarse & sugary fine —
were hers & mine

& now with grace in my arms
lifting her from wheelchair
& gently depositing her on grassy patch, rim of
Cooper Lake

but couldn't lift her from a kneeling position
& couldn't suppress a chubby

(may Christ have mercy
on my twisted soul)

& G.'s poser:
*Could you justify your life & work in 25 words
or less?*

Yes, like so:

under high-
tension wire

yellow
flower

keeping a
low profile

8.30

at Joe's, he got a massage from a misogynist

then came home to witness the birth of a parking lot

ordeal by phone, ragweed headache, bloated feeling after eating

but mom looks 20 years younger

dad wants to know if art is theft

no, *good* art is theft

after they leave I'm able to hear the silence between objects

I'm able to be there as

barely percussive

a puff of milkweed

grazes against the

wind chimes

9.4

parkway mantra:

NOT A COP ON THE TACONIC
NOT A COP ON THE TACONIC

but when I get there, dinner is death by daikon

& now with her asleep, I find a
flashlight, wobble out to

the compost heap, to pinpoint
in the dim unsteady flicker a

sextet of red efts
squiggling in the midden

where mold, methodical & blue,
deconstructs the text of yesterday's

bread

9.12

looking at his paintings, the dense accretion of oils &
collaged elements—temperature gauges, matchbook covers,
nuts and bolts and washers, magazine
illustrations, paper clips, even a
couple of condoms—and
still recognizably a face, as all our faces remain in
the rain of unremitting paraphernalia, the accumulated
tonnage of iron filings attracted by memory's magnet,
the miracle that our faces are not effaced, our faces
not obliterated by love's flotsam, memory's jetsam

but how does a poet go postal?

eruption of silence?

sets minnows (or little fish?) in motion, by passing the
shadow of hand across the water . . . arrowed thoughts
emanating from shadow head, & scattering

"Don't laugh, it took seven days to paint that!"

& nearly as long
to watch it deteriorate,

the old neighborhood
in river mist, shawled
in its falling, crumbling
into its element, mycelial
poetry of moldy roofs &
furbished churches

9.24

her fortune cookie:
Be very careful tonight

she looks me over & laughs

"What do women want?" she
mimics, & suddenly I'm crumbling

into the car, rusty
harbinger of autumn

the drive a blur
from there to not-there

in one here & out the other

9.30

an I of geese going south

strange geraniums
standing in the rain
singing from Mental Health Songbook

through the wood, followed by a rowdydow of crows, to the old graveyard shaded by three great maples and grandfather catalpa, the corvids blackly swooping over, barking to the stones, to this one with its blotch of lichen, white-gray flares of ash on darker charcoal, Wilhelminus F. France, Nov. 29, 1867

partially enflamed maple:
first tints of past tense

10.14

migratory mob of birds de-
camped in a circle of trees
around the house, a spectacle
awesome & deafening, an almost
malevolent event of the first
magnitude

plus ca change, plus c'est le mime shows

& yet each day a gift

each gift a myriad lives

his girlfriend has that certain *fermez la bouche*

let's shed
these colors

& slip into
something a

little more
rigorous

10.15

autumn hems mount tremper

a mountain brooklet trips along, mordant water gossiping to rocks

a chainsaw effectively quells the conversation

•

all day, I tingle with shame

a sort of barely tangible horripilation of the aura

•

all danced out in the wrinkled creek

a maple leaf goes rafting into the afterlife

10.23

spilling its
deep red heart
into the streets

emotional explosions of

oak, sassafras, maple
& native beech, & tears of

letting go, wanting
to let go freely as

each red leaf, unhooking itself
in splendid surrender from each
black tree

Sex with you
she says to me
is like missing the boat!

charred orange, weathered red, blunt mustard, slow brown

crumbling up the hill,   & wrinkling down

11.3

most unfelicitous dyspepsia

I'd show you this to assuage your grief
this wizened wisteria leaf
in the small, bushy beard
of a bonsai juniper

cigarette placed in skeletal teeth of dead possum at roadside

fired veins
& kindling hearts

It is only desire
parts me from the
tree

11.10

oaks uncloak
hickories unzip

entropy shoots from the hip
   shoots *itself* in the hip

(I haven't been cured of romantic obsessiveness; I've just been cured — for now — of taking chances)

aah but who dances
   with each freed
         leaf?

the owners released from having
the lovers released from loving

11.18

the memory of eros: honey in the bank

& on the piano, gossamer runs with guts

droplets of blood, those ubiquitous red
berries, only color in beige November bleak-
scape, save the partial green (dishabille) of
snow-swathed firs

but damn it, does it all have to be so decorative?
apparently, yes — e.g.,

first
snowfall
& the forest
pristine as faerie

(wrong way
on Moon Haw
Road, snow-mottled
hollow in smoky shadow
of Peekamoose)

C'mon, who said *pristine*?
The genius loci of power lines?

11.24

ah, this life

we ate it
with undivided
Tibetan attention

or so I'd like my readers to believe

not hinting for an instant
that all my adamant phantoms

— iron ghosts forged in apparitional foundries of memory & desire —

all of them so thoroughly distracted
me that I couldn't distinguish head
from rectum,

sex from text, or
masturbating from

collaborating with myself

12.5

talking, what a wonderful way to die

she hangs up & semantically, I'm in the middle of some
nowhere

the neighborhood merely splendent with levitated sleighs,
fiberglass santas, plastic magi, polyurethane snowmen

the real season elsewhere

what's the point of storm & stress if it can't be recollected
in tranquility, with maybe a bit of Slivovitz & a Tylenol
?

ants explore the lavatory floor, patterns of squares & rectangles
endlessly replicated, & the ants endlessly replicated, each a
model for every other ant

& on the dresser a brown recluse, nested in her gregarious bra

12.10

Occurring in time:
high cry of a circling hawk,
cold clink of a chime.

But behind or below them, look:
the bed in whose shimmer time is dreamed,
this trickling brook.

12.18

hail to the eye who notices that

of a junked
lump of tires
snow makes a mound
of oreos

Venus & Jupiter bright as child prodigies

& down below the
legislators nodding,
somnolent, or just plain
indifferent to trees,
creeks, mountains, &
other impediments to
progress

none of them working as hard
as this reedman, coaxing a raw
compendium of ideas from sweat
& metal

jazz the blue juice
the force that through the green fuse
drives the blower

12.30

these jottings, these marks
because the year is like a dying friend or lover, it
wants us to think of it after it's gone

Pleiades icily singing a cappella
Orion a lost piper, tilting in a starry kilt
to skirl across the sky

I love to see her wicked smile through
the red webs of her hair streaming over
my face, smothering me in auburn

& now she calls me to feed the animals

& whatever the years bring
there will always be animals,
& animals more proficient at
handling heavy machinery to
feed them

& already the year is a place I can't
remember, a bookstore in ashes, a bridge
whose cables & stanchions are blurred by
fog, connecting terras infirma to terras
incognita

evening star a perfect beauty, perfectly removed

A NOTE ON THE POEMS

The 42 poems in this book were culled from a 365-poem opus titled *One Year.* Each poem in *One Year* was composed according to the following method: I would take a day—say, January 18—and, sifting through more than 25 years of journals, extract everything that was entered on that date (thoughts, reportage, dreams, conversations, overheard remarks, passages copied from books I was reading, etc.). Then I would isolate clusters of material, combine and recombine them, amplifying and further atomizing the fragments and finally whittling them down to no more than one page of text. So while everything that "happens" in a given poem did indeed transpire on its given date, that date is unmoored in time, representing many years and as many places and circumstances—ergo, the "she" who appears in the first line of a particular poem is not necessarily the same "she" who appears in the next line.

ABOUT THE AUTHOR

Mikhail Horowitz is the author of *Big League Poets* (City Lights, 1978) and *The Opus of Everything in Nothing Flat* (Red Hill/Outloud, 1993). His poetry, short plays, and artwork have been widely published in the small-press world and featured in *City Lights Journal*, *The Stiffest of the Corpse*, *Into the Temple of Baseball*, *Laugh Lines*, and other anthologies, as well as in the *New York Times*. His performance work, with jazz and acoustic musicians and/or with his longtime partner Gilles Malkine, can be heard on a dozen CDs, including *The Blues of the Birth* (Sundazed Records) and the anthology album *Bring It On Home*, Vol. II (Columbia Records). He lives in the woods north of Saugerties, New York, with the printmaker Carol Zaloom and three cats. His day gig is impersonating an editor at Bard College.